Old Bramley & Stanningley

Paul Chrystal

Going through the locks on the Leeds Liverpool Canal at Bramley Fall Woods. The stretch of the canal between Leeds and Gargrave was cut by 1777, and the entirety of the canal by 1816. It is 127 miles long and crosses the Pennines with the help of 91 locks on the main line. The canal took almost 50 years to complete having been held up by wars in the American colonies and Europe. The most important cargo was coal, with over a million tons per year being delivered to Liverpool in the 1860s, but once the canal was fully open, receipts for carrying other merchandise matched those of coal. The heavy industry along its route, together with the decision to build the canal with broad locks, ensured that the Leeds and Liverpool competed successfully with the railways throughout the 19th century and remained open through the 20th century.

Text © Paul Chrystal, 2021.
First published in the United Kingdom, 2021,
by Stenlake Publishing Ltd.,
54-58 Mill Square,
Catrine, Ayrshire,
KA5 6RD

Telephone: 01290 551122
www.stenlake.co.uk

ISBN 9781840338959

The publishers regret that they cannot supply copies of any pictures featured in this book.

Acknowledgement

I am indebted to John Barker of the Bramley History Society and Friends of a War Memorial for Bramley for the books and pamphlets he provided. Much of the information here comes from the research and photography produced over the years by these two organisations – they were especially valuable given that all libraries were closed while I researched this book. Thanks also to Terry Shires and John Warr of Shires Organ Pipes Ltd for permission to use the photograph of John Warr, and for explaining what a rounding block is and does. Josh Flint at Leeds Libraries Archives and Harriet Harmer at West Yorkshire Archive Service are also due my thanks.

Left: The rear entrance and yard of 113 Town Street, a through terraced property, on 26th August 1963. The Lavan family's clothes hang on washing lines stretched across the yard while ladders, a chair and a clothes horse are stacked by the door. A tricycle stands in the middle of the yard and a pram is on the right. There is an empty pigeon coop with an open door above the door in the corner.

Introduction

The name Bramley derives from 'Bram', the Old English word for broom plant, and 'ley', a clearing. Others maintain, however, that it is a place inhabited by a man called Bram (Parsons, *History of Leeds, &c*, Vol1, p.194). There is no evidence of prehistoric occupation of the site of Bramley and signs of Roman presence are limited to three coins from the 3rd or 4th centuries AD. The early settlement probably developed on the arrival of the Anglo-Saxons in the 7th or 8th centuries AD. The first record of Bramley comes in the 1086 *Domesday Book* where it is listed as "Brameleia" and "Bramelie". The area is described as 'waste' after the devastation of the Harrying of the North shock and awe. People mentioned include: Alsige; Arnbiorn; Arnketil; Dunstan; Escelf; Gamal; Healfdene; Ilbert de Lacy; Leofnoth; Morfari; Ralph; Ramkel; Sindi; Stenulf; Thorsten; Vestarr. Nearby Kirkstall Abbey, founded 1172, owned land around Bramley until the Dissolution. William de Poitou and Adam de Reinville were among the first to benefit from grants of Bramley land to Kirkstall – the latter's extending from Newlay to Armley Ridge. The abbott of the abbey was Bramley's Lord of the Manor. The monks set up granges at Whitecote and at Hill Top. After the Dissolution Archbishop Cranmer took possession; then Elizabeth I and later the Duke of Montague and the Brudenels, Earls of Cardigan.

The village pump and trough are all that remain as reminders of Bramley Village Green which was surrounded by medieval cottages and yards. The Green was also home to the stocks, pillory and an 8ft pillar which commemorated the holding of Leeds Market here during the plague of 1644-45: it was thought that holding the market on higher ground would be safer – nevertheless, 20% of the Leeds population died within six months. In 1798, when Town Street was being widened, the pillar was damaged. Stone from it was later used in the rebuilding of the walls of Stocks Hill in 1827, an early act of civic vandalism which sadly was to be repeated on a prodigious scale some 130 years later. Subsequently Bramley developed in a linear progression along today's Town Street.

In 1663 the Hearth Tax records reveal that there were 56 Bramley people possessing 93 hearths or stoves between them, thus giving a population of around 280. There would have been a number of exemptions due to poverty adding perhaps a further 70 persons (Benjamin Wilson, *Our Village: a Sketch of the History and Progress of Bramley*, Bramley 1860).

The monks of the abbey established a chapel of ease at Bramley dedicated to St. Margaret the Virgin of Antioch; it is believed to have stood near Town Street, probably on open land that is adjacent to the Old Unicorn public house and was enlarged in 1836, then closed down in 1861 to be replaced by a new church dedicated to St. Peter, built in 1863.

Some of the oldest surviving buildings in Bramley are at 112 Lower Town Street where the remains of a timber-framed aisled hall dating to *c.*1500 can be seen. The timber framing was encased in stone in the 17th or 18th century to produce the grade II listed building that we see today. Bramley Fall, which is in the public park and is now covered in trees, was once a busy quarry that provided a great deal of building stone in the late 18th and early 19th centuries with which many of the historic buildings in Bramley were built including a canal-side wharf. A later quarry here supplied road stone. A 1771 engraving shows Stocks Hill; this is where the main well was and so it naturally became a focal point for the settlement of Bramley where voters waited to hear the results of local elections, and there was singing at Christmas and Whitsun. Horses were still drinking from the trough near the well in the 1920s.

In the 19th century industry arrived and with it the population explosion largely required to staff the woollen textile industry in the early part of the century and boot making and engineering industries in later years. In the first quarter of the 19th century Bramley's population increased almost threefold mainly due to the industrialisation of numerous cottage industries. 1801– 2,565 inhabitants; 1831– 7,039; 1861– 8,691; 1901– 17,229. In 1851 half of the population was born outside Bramley. Clothiers were leaving Leeds on account of the high rents and coming to places like Bramley where rents were markedly lower.

Crane building was developed by Joseph Booth & Bros. Ltd at their Union Foundry and Iron Works in Rodley from 1847. They started with pioneering the steam crane, upgrading to electricity in the early 20th century. Competition came with Thomas Smith & Sons (Rodley) Ltd who originally made wooden cranes from 1820; their electricity was switched on in 1900 with the first electric crane delivered two years later.

By the 1830s there were 20 mills and other works within Bramley: of these 16 were woollen mills. One, Elmfield Mill in Back Lane, was famous for its telescopic chimney. The Yorkshire cloth industry had begun in the reign of Edward III (1327-77) when he granted licence to two Flemish artisans – Willielmus and Hankeinus de Brabant to settle in York and start cloth making there. He attracted other migrant weavers, dyers or fullers with the offer of royal protection. By the reign of Henry VIII Leland tells us that Leeds was 'standing much by clothing'. By the 1660s Charles II saw that the manufacture of cloth in Yorkshire was contributing nicely to the national revenues and gave protection against the charlatans defrauding the manufacturers and the royal customs. Leeds went from strength to strength in the 18th century supported by new technologies, culminating in the steam loom patented by Edward Cartwright in 1787. Benjamin Gott of Armley was one of the first to take these developments on board locally. The quantity of cloth milled in Yorkshire went from 26,000 pieces in 1726 to 450,000 pieces in 1800.

Bramley obviously enjoyed a share in this. The first mill was Ross Mill which opened before 1794; the first Jenny was spun by Thomas Clough at the Duck-cote; the first scribbling machine was at Ross Mill; the first steam mill was Hough Mill built around 1798.

There was a tannery on Waterloo Lane which has also submitted to the council's wrecking ball; then there was the world famous church organ works that became Shires Organ Pipes Ltd.

Bramley Mills

Aire Vale Dyeworks; Airedale Mills; Allen Brigg Mill (1830); Arrowvale Mill; Bath Lane Mill; Bell Isle Mill (1807); Bramley Mill; Britannia Mill; Broad Lane Mill; Cape Mills (1799); Catherine Mills; Company Mills (1794); Craven Mills; Elmfield Mill (1831); Empire Mills; Hough End Mills (1797); Low Mill; Moss Bridge Works; New Mills (1804); Prospect Works; Ross Mills (<1794); St. Catherine's Mill; Spring Valley Mills; Springfield Mill; St. Helens (1802); St. John's (1873); Swinnow Grange Mill (1857); Swinnow Lane Mill; Swinnow Moor (1835); Town End Mills; Victoria Mill (1837); Waterloo Mill (1816); Wellington Mill (1823); West Field Mills.

Broad Lane Mills were occupied by Wolsey Ltd, one of twelve Wolsey factories employing 3,000 workers around the country. Bramley alone had 400 Wolsey employees in the '30s spinning 2m lbs of material each year. They were unique in that they did French Drawing and Worsted Mule Spinning and were famous for their socks, underwear and swimwear.

In the early 20th century the industrial landscape was more diverse, with rhubarb growing, organ making, tanning, crane building, jam making and quarrying. This is how manufacturing by type in percentage terms in Bramley looked in 1939 and 1989:

Manufacturing Type	Percentage 1939	Percentage 1989
Food and drink	5%	3%
Textiles	39%	9%
Clothing and curtains	2%	9%
Wood and furniture	11%	7%
Chemicals	13%	2%
Engineering	18%	25%
Paper, plastic containers and printing	5%	28%
Miscellaneous	10%	17%
Total:	100% from 61 firms in 1939	100% from 57 firms in 1989

[Source: Anthony Silson, *Bramley: Half a Century of Change*, Leeds, 1991]

By the 1920s the village had developed, but its limits only extended as far as the railway station and Hough End; the Globe at the top of Town Street was as good as any marker for the end of Bramley civilisation. Newlay Lane was a country lane and the fields around still had bucolic names like 'Buttercup and Daisy Fields'. These were still the days of outside toilets in the back yard – sometimes shared – with no bathroom, never enough bedrooms, a network of ginnels, zinc baths, possets and mangles. Outside toilets persisted until 1969.

Commercially, Bramley was blessed with a large number of shops for its size. The majority were on Town Street and Stanningley Road which between them were home to about 140 out of a total of 217 in 1939. Of these 40 were butchers and greengrocers, and 31 clothes and footwear. By comparison, the number of shops on the two roads in 1989 was 56 out of a town total of 145 with 20 butchers and greengrocers and ten clothes and footwear shops.

The 1960s and 1970s saw Bramley blighted by an unsympathetic and inappropriate mindless redevelopment which wrecked the historic integrity of the area and irreparably ruined the appearance and the character of the town and was condemned as one of the least sensitive such programmes in Yorkshire. Nowadays much of what remains of historical Bramley is protected by the Bramley Town Conservation Area, which is concentrated in and around Bramley Hough Lane and Bramley Town Street.

Right: This firm was established by James Jepson Binns (1855-1929) of Warrel's Grove in 1880. Binns was initially apprenticed to the Leeds firm of Radcliffe and Sagar, and from about 1873 to 1880 he worked for Abbott and Smith, latterly as head voicer. It was here that he was challenged on a matter of organ building by the eminent Leeds musician J.W. Broughton. who had a Schulze chamber organ in his music room, which was tuned by Mr. Binns on behalf of Messrs Abbott & Co. According to the Revd Theodore Brocklehurst, writing in *The Organ* of July 1929 Mr. Broughton became so interested in young Binns, that learning of his great ambition to start organ building on his own account, said to him: "If you can make a pipe and put it into one of the diapason stops so that I cannot detect the difference between your pipe and the rest, I think I might be able to put you in the way of starting." When Binns successfully resolved the issue, Broughton found investors to stump up money to help start up the Bramley Organ Works run by Binns in 1880. By the First World War he had built more than 500 organs, some 200 of them in Yorkshire. He also exported organs to South Africa, the West Indies and Jerusalem. A good example of his work is at Queens' College, Cambridge. Binns' work is characterised by sturdy design and workmanship, and the solid construction of the organs earned them the nickname 'battleship Binns'. Demolition of the works and a redevelopment of the surrounding back-to-back terraced houses began after the 1950s.

Bramley Recreation Ground preceded Bramley Park and originally had a high stone wall all around and a six feet herbaceous border. There were numerous shelters, a bowling green and tennis courts. The monument (now in the rose garden in what is Bramley Park) celebrates the Reverend John Gott who was the vicar of St. Peter's Bramley from 1866 to 1873, after which he moved to Leeds Parish Church. In 1868 John Gott married Harriot Mary Maitland, set up a parish magazine and formed a church council consisting of clergy, churchwardens and laymen. Such a council is believed to be the first of its kind in England.

An Edwardian scene in the park. The grounds were laid out and planted in 1872; the bandstand and old man's shelter on the left were higher up on the slope with a turfed recreation ground below for children to play. There is an underground reservoir at the highest point of the park. Two 'Speaker' stones offered a platform for anyone who wished to thunder forth. The bandstand was replaced by the Coronation Villa. Today the park offers wide open spaces on a hillside, sports pitches, tennis courts, a bowling green, a children's playground, the war memorial and a rose garden. Annual events such as Bramley Carnival and a fireworks display take place here.

This photograph shows the red brick shelter in the middle of Bramley Park, built on the site of the old bandstand. It was not built as a shelter as such but as a 'Wendy' house for children to play and learn housecraft skills in and was erected to celebrate the coronation of King George VI on 12th May 1937. The single storey building offered a dining room, sitting room, kitchen and toilet.

St. Margaret's Church was off Town Street, Stocks Hill behind the Old Unicorn. A small chapel was built on this site in 1631 which was enlarged and rebuilt around 1729. Benjamin Wilson tells us that the oldest gravestone in the burial ground is dated 1673 and cautions us all that 'here lyeth the body of Catherine, the wife of William Vevers, of Bramley…House and riches are the inheritance of fathers, but a prudent wife is from the Lord' *Prov*. xix. 14. In 1717 the first baptism here, of Sarah Parker, was recorded; the first marriage is in 1724 between John Naylor and Mary Craven of Bramley. July 1728 was a tragic time for Joshua Burton: on the 24th his three sons (Abraham, Isaac and Jacob) were baptised and his wife, Mary, was buried. The 28th saw Isaac and Jacob buried; Abraham followed them before the end of the month. By 1861 the church was deemed unfit for purpose and was demolished although the spire was retained. A new church, St. Peter's, was built, just to the north of the old St. Margaret's site. The Newlay area of Bramley has been home to three churches called St. Margaret's over the years. The first was the 1631 church opposite the Abbey Inn at the bottom of Pollard Lane; it was replaced by a bigger church further up Pollard Lane, which was itself replaced in 1958 by the present church.

The foundation stone for St. Peter's Church was laid in 1861 with the consecration taking place on 9th July 1863 and the service given by the Lord Bishop of Ripon. The church seats 1,325 people and is built of sandstone. It is an example of Geometric Gothic style and cost £4,500. The land was donated by the 7th Earl of Cardigan. It replaced the old St.Margaret's Church which was reputed to have been built by monks from Kirkstall Abbey and demolished in 1861. St. Peter's Church was partially rebuilt in the late 1970s and the original spire was incorporated into the new-build. It is Grade II listed.

Zion Baptist Church was formed in 1796 by a group of Christian believers in Bedworth near Coventry who followed Jesus Christ and his teachings, with the Bible as the sole authority in all matters of their faith and service. In Bramley the Zionists started worshipping in a barn at the top of Outgang; in 1832 they opened a library. The original chapel in Hough Lane dating from 1808 became too small for the growing congregation but it continued in use as a schoolroom until new Sunday Schools were built in 1896. Around 1830 the Sunday School numbered more than 400 attendees. Joseph Askwith was the old chapel's first pastor: after 20 years service in the army he came back to Bramley, his native village, and, deeply affected with the spiritual destitution of his local flock, began preaching in private houses; for nine years he preached in a barn, which was hired for the purpose, where he met with considerable success. The replacement stone-built Italianate style Zion Baptist Chapel in Hough Lane pictured here cost £2,500. At the inaugural services in 1846, led by the Reverend James MacPherson, £405 6 shillings 10 pence was collected towards the cost. The chapel could boast a theatre group: the Zion Dramatic Players which had links with Leeds Operatic and Dramatic Society. Apart from the usual dominoes, draughts, billiards and cricket, Zion offered lawn tennis. In 1870, when the organ was installed, 72 members of the congregation, half the total congregation, disapproved; they voted with their feet and left to form the Salem.

Salem means peace. The concept of family is vital for Baptists; the church is not so much a particular place or building, but rather a family of believers, committed to Christ, to one another and to the service of God in the world. At the end of the First World War the toll on the men of Great Britain was so great that it left many families, particularly children, somewhat vulnerable in all sorts of ways. The wealthier ladies of the town, therefore, set up the first 'Babies Welcome' in the Salem Chapel schoolroom, paid the rent and bought the equipment. A nurse and health visitor were engaged and it opened with 119 babies, rising to 417 within one year. This amazing piece of pre-NHS child welfare moved to Town End in 1921. Bramley's Salem Baptist Chapel was in Westover Road; William Smith, joiner and funeral director, and his sons built the adjoining Sunday School. The Rev. A. Ashworth, pastor at Zion for fourteen years, became the first pastor at Salem, where he continued until his death in 1885. In 1897 Rev. James Wilkinson, who had been for eight years minister at Zion, became pastor of the Salem Church. The organ was installed in 1901. There was also the Tin Tabernacle in Westover Road run by the Church of the Nazarene.

Town Street about 1900. The shops on the right are A. Fairbanks, stationers, ('cheap') printers and postcard sellers – they had a branch in Pudsey; and Walkers, boot makers. The domed building on the left is the Midland Bank after the archway which leads to Hobson's Yard. Other shops and buildings in Town Street down the years included the police station, opened in 1857 and affectionately known as the 'bobby hole'; Broad Lane School; the Globe; Hustler's Electric Fisheries; Meadow Dairies; Maypole Dairies; Peter Haley decorators; Whitham's off licence which also sold fireworks and Spinks Odds and Ends – off-cuts from the Spinks Liquorice Allsorts factory in Leeds; Jesse Stephenson, grocers; Lister's Pork Shop on the corner of Bell Lane; Lambert's bakers and confectioners; Dales the greengrocers; two chemists: Boots and Hopkinsons – the latter offering a baby weighing service; the Public Benefit shoe shop; Thompsons cake shop – Mr. Thompson lectured throughout the UK and abroad on baking – his classic book on fancy cakes and pastries was a bestseller, not least in Austria and Switzerland where they know a thing or two about pastries; Neville's sweets, off licence and tobacconists; Blenkinsops, greengrocers, famous for his Lucky Bags and Don Bradman's Boundary Hits.

Town Street at the junction with Hough Lane and Waterloo Lane. Some rather erudite signage at Ross Brothers on the right: 'Nil Simile' is Latin for 'nothing's the same' or 'nothing like it' and was a brand of shoes and handbags – they are still trading today. The brand was acquired in 2000 by Equity Shoes, saving it from liquidation. Nil Simile specialises in very narrow and very wide fittings. Tram 275 is arriving at Bramley. The Zebra advertised on the tram was one of many metal polishes (Brasso, Zebo etc), lavatory cleaners (Harpic), starches and laundry blue (Reckitt's Blue) manufactured by Reckitt & Sons in Hull. They still trade today, in the same Hull factory, now as Reckitt Benckiser plc, the world's biggest household cleaning product manufacturer. Zebra was big business in the days when people religiously cleaned and polished their fire grates and stoves.

The tram from Rodley is advertising the Empire Palace Theatre in Briggate. Trams to Rodley from Leeds started on 9th July 1906; the track had been laid by unemployed labour. Due to the severe gradient on the route at Whitecote Hill a speed limit of 4mph was imposed on this stretch. The advertising hoardings on the right are promoting Royal Enfield bicycles amongst other things. Moriah Methodist Chapel was down an alley (the Crescent) off Upper Town Street; Bramley Moriah Chapel was one of three Methodist chapels close to each other, the others being Wesley Place and Brunswick. In 1956 these three congregations came together to form the Trinity Methodist Society. "Moriah" is the name of the mountain in the Bible where Abraham offered up his son Isaac; it means "God provides". Mori + yah ("yah" = God). And that is why some churches are called "(Mt) Moriah Church". Bramley's Moriah described themselves as 'Pioneers of Healthy Recreation for Young People'. Witt's the printers was run by two sisters, and printed the *Bramley Weekly Advertiser*; also Steve Miller cobblers; Tommy Bennett's garage; tram sheds; Good Shepherd School and Babies Welcome; Ernest Lawson's garage, who donated a dilapidated car to Bramley National School for driving lessons; and the Yorkshire Bank on the corner of Hough Lane.

At the corner of Pudsey Road and Henconner Lane. Hough End was home to Gibson's Tannery and Boyes and Helliwell's Mill. The Peggy Well spring was here with its beck as were Billy Mitchell's market garden, Park Spring Quarries, Wadsworth's piggeries, Hough End Primitive Chapel, the Beulah pub and Binks' rhubarb fields. The blackboard shutter at the grocer's is advertising mineral waters. In the late 19th century Fry's was the UK's leading manufacturer of chocolate; they were later to merge with Cadbury's. Both companies embraced advertising while the third force in the industry, Rowntree's, took a much more cautious and low-key approach to marketing – sales and growth suffered as a result. Also on Hough End Lane was a grand house called The Grange. Hough End Bridge which spanned Farley Beck eventually became part of the ring road.

Before developers and the Leeds ring road barged in Bramley was very much a rural delight of a place, as witnessed by Mary Gawthorpe, the suffragette, socialist, trade unionist and editor, who described her experience living and working as a teacher at Hough Lane School between 1905 and 1907: 'Bramley was an oasis of peace, and old established centre of homes and living yet within the city bounds… from our kitchen at Warrel's Mount we looked out on open fields. The walk to school was almost rural in its calm'. – Mary Gawthorpe (1962), *Up Hill to Holloway*, Michigan, p.189.

This is Whitecote, meaning either white hut or white fold. The carriages and wagon works of C. Binns is in the background. Whitecote could get its name from the White Coats – those elements of Charles I's army who camped around here at Warley Camp under General Warley in the Civil War. The enemy, the Roundheads were dubbed the Red Coats. Cromwell's Roundheads were encamped at Cleverley, probably in preparation for one of the battles which was fought near Bradford.

Whitecote Fisheries – a fish and chip shop – was at 29 Coppy Lane here. This business was preceded in the 1940s by the 'Original Fisheries' and Sheldon's fish and chip shop.

The antiquarian Benjamin Wilson was the first person to write a history of Bramley, published in 1860: *Our Village: a sketch of the history and progress of Bramley during seven centuries*, J. Dawson, Bramley. He donated his collection to Leeds City Museum, including a witch's bottle found in Whitecote in 1861. In the very early days a witch's bottle contained the victim's (the person on whom a spell was put on), urine, hair or nail clippings, or red thread from sprite traps. Later witch bottles were filled with rosemary, needles and pins, and red wine.

Elmfield Mill, Back Lane, Bramley. Deeds for the hand loom weaving mill date it to 1688; there is also a stone bearing the inscription, "Wm Turner and Haner, his wife, A.D. 1732". It was once called Lister's High Mill to differentiate it from Lister's Low Mill, at Hough End, which was also owned by J. Lister. It later became the Elmfield Mill Manufacturing Company manufacturing vicuña, a South American camelid related to the alpaca. A fountain (originally outside Leeds Town Hall) was installed at Elmfield House; it was set so that the water began to play when the engine at the mill started, so the mill owner knew precisely when work had begun. The mill has a unique telescoping chimney which could be raised and lowered as needed.

Bramley Baths – 'a jewel in Leeds' leisure crown', according to *The Guardian*. Going to the baths in the 19th century was a completely different experience from a trip to the local leisure centre and swimming pool today. Then it was much more about public hygiene and health. After numerous outbreaks of cholera and other infectious diseases in the 1800s, something had to be done to improve the sanitation of the country, so, mindful that it was finally accepted that improved hygiene promoted better health, local corporations in the early 20th century started to build public baths, swimming pools and wash houses. These were predominantly in areas of back-to-back houses and cottages where water was shared at a communal, often fetid, pump or where it was difficult for people to heat water, or enjoy a modicum of privacy. The picture shows Leeds champions at the baths – both boys and girls. In the winter months the baths were used for dancing – a popular social venue in the area. The original pool hall surrounded on three sides by a balcony is still there as are the wooden changing cubicles based around the pool side, underneath the balcony. Men changed on the right hand side of the pool, women on the left.

Bramley Baths is the only remaining Edwardian bath-house in Leeds and is Grade II listed. It first opened as a pool and public bath-house in 1904, enabling local residents to wash, swim and use the Russian Steam Baths, fashionable with the Edwardians as a health-giving indulgence. The baths were built on the site of a steel foundry. The chimney is a landmark across Leeds and was built using 8,000 Kirkstall bricks. Russian banyas, баня, or saunas/steam baths, are a quintessential Russian experience; they have been steam-cleaning people for centuries. Maybe not what you'd expect in Bramley? Banyas usually have three rooms: a steam room, a washing room and an entrance room (предбанник 'predbannik'). The entrance room or pre-bath, has pegs to hang your clothes on, and benches to rest on. There is a whole culture and ritual surrounding banyas; here are a few of them: get naked; do say 'yes' to a good thrashing from a stranger and offer to return the favour – gentle lashing with a wad of birch tree branches, or venik, is good for the skin; banya temperatures often exceed 93 degrees C so don't drink water, drink tea.

For a small charge a bath could be enjoyed, the small room being at the bather's disposal for 20-30 minutes. The waiting area provided here has deck chairs. To the right a bath cubicle can be seen.

Houghley Ghyll, one of the many ginnels in Bramley is unusual in that it is lined with trees on both sides. The origin of the ginnel is disputed: some say they were the routes for pack horses; that they were just medieval back lanes, or that they were footpaths walled at the time of the Enclosure Acts. These walls were three to four feet wide and could be up to six or seven feet high with many a stile and stoop to keep the cattle out. The Long Ginnel was the longest, extending from Stanningley Road to Bell Lane and giving onto many of the yards.

Yards too were a common feature of the town. This 1960 photograph shows the back of semi-derelict stone properties in Newcastle Place taken from Harrison Yard. On the left are 22 and 24 Harrison Yard and at right angles to them, 17, 15 and 13 Newcastle Place. There was Ivy Yard in Lower Town Street opposite the Star and Garter; Farrar's Yard, Turner's Yard, Spetch Yard, Ebenezer Place, Patchett Place, Barker's Yard, Mirfield Yard and Hayley's Yard – the only one to survive. Wilson's Yard was home to Bramley's Mechanics' Institute founded 1845 with its 989 volume library. Up to eight cottages would be shoehorned into the yards which were a throwback to the cottage hand loom weaving days and a microcosm of society in general: the slums that were the cottages were dominated by 'the big house' in which the much better off and better educated resident often gave his name to the yard and expected to be looked up to. He, of course, would not share the ash pit or the midden. Rents for the cottages were 3/6d in 1918.

A yard at the back of Town Street giving access to the Sanitas Steam Laundry with covered delivery cart parked outside. The first steam-powered laundries in England were built in 1825; unfortunately they had a tendency to rip the linen to shreds: we had to wait until the textile manufacturers resolved the problems of large-scale linen handling before you got your laundry back in one piece. There was also the Sunshine Laundry in Mirfield Yard. Stephenson's fish and chip shop in Town Street was built on the site of a building known as the Mangle Shop – that was where you took your sheets and other washing to be mangled.

The Sanitas Steam Laundry at 126 Town Street looking towards Stocks Hill. *Sanitas* is Latin for 'health' or 'soundness of body or mind'. In this context, though, 'Sanitas' is a safe but powerful disinfectant derived from the eucalyptus tree: it has no unpleasant smell, is non-toxic and colourless.

Hollybush Primary School, Broad Lane, was previously called Broad Lane Board School, Broad Lane County Primary School and then Broad Lane Middle School. It opened on 1st October 1900 for 650 pupils and catered for boys and girls. There was a workshop at the rear for boys' 'manual training'. Board schools were the first state-run schools: local Boards could raise funds from a rate, build and run non-denominational schools where existing voluntary provision was inadequate. They could subsidise church schools and where appropriate pay the fees of the poorest children. If they deemed it necessary, they could create a by-law making attendance compulsory between ages 5-13. They did not offer religious education, other than simple Bible reading. The photo is of May Day at Broad Lane in the 1960s. Other pre Second World War schools in Bramley included Christ the King, Good Shepherd (opened 1896 for 5-7 year olds), Hough Lane Board School (1877), Bramley Church School (opened in 1850) and Bramley National. This was replaced from 1865-1871 by a Middle Class School (Middle School) inspirationally offering book-keeping, Latin, French, German and music as well as the usual fare. Hough Lane was built for 560 pupils on the top of a hill in 1877 as it was believed that it was healthy up there. It was extended in 1900 when girls were allowed in, bringing the total number of pupils to 561.

This photo shows staff at G.B. Simpson's Whitegate Farm between Town Street and Stanningley Road behind St. Catherine's Mill in Cat Babbleton getting ready for the first of the day's two milk deliveries. Milk was originally delivered to the door in 2 ½ gallon churns where it was measured out into the housewife's jug – one pint or ½ pint twice a day (no refrigeration then). The fridge came in the 1930s along with a mechanical bottle washer which obviated manual washing. Mr. Simpson later moved to Moorside Farm. Groceries and wet fish also came by horses and carts. Mothers believed that the fumes from the gas tar cart cured croup so children were often made to follow it round to inhale the fumes. Other farms included Bradley Hill Farm which belonged to the Drivers on the Leeds and Bradford Road; the farm run by Minnie and George Emmett near Broad Lane; and Warrington Bros. farming off Elder Road, Ducky Hills – Duck Cote Farm? – and near Bramley Station. These were mainly dairy but Bell's Farm in Raynville Road focused on pigs. There was a mixed farm behind Yates Mill: Pepper Lane Farm in Cat Babbleton. Rhubarb too was big business around Bramley with more than a third of all the Leeds forcing sheds here, and Leeds was a market leader in UK and global rhubarb.

Taken 7th April 1960 this stone building with padlocked wooden doors is in Barker's Place at the back of 8 Bell Lane with washing and sidecar bereft of motor bike. From the late 19th century into the 20th century it was used by painter and decorator James Albert Naylor as a store for his ladders. Mr. Naylor ran his business from 271 Upper Town Street. He specialised in painting chapels and churches and was skilled in gilding and stencilling. His work could be seen at the Moriah Chapel and the Ebenezer and Wesley Place Chapels. He was also responsible for the original decoration of Armley Public Library, or the Free Library as it was then known. Barker's Place was named after the Barkers – a woollen manufacturing family who built the houses here.

E & W Lawson's garage at Town End by the Scarborough junction of Stanningley Road – the long-established firm of motor agents included showrooms, repair shop and pumps and was a successful business built up in the 1930s. Lawson's owned other premises at the junction of Half Mile Lane and Stanningley Town Street. Other commercial enterprises around Stanningley Road included Turner's, making tanning machinery; Tap & Toothill, printers; Binns Organ Works (burnt down), Victoria Mills on Elder Road (burnt down); and Britannia Mill on Swinnow Road. By 1930 Turner's were employing over 300 people and making over 100 different types of machinery for the tanning industry.

Before 1960 there were old stone-built weaver's cottages in Town End Yard off Lower Town Street. These properties would originally have had workshops on the upper storeys. Number 15 was a boot manufacturers in 1888 called T. & J.H. Stewart. In *Yards of Bramley*, a Bramley History Society publication, a former resident remembers the flagstone floor in the kitchen as being very uneven and often very wet with water seeping up. Bramley tram sheds were here at the end of Stanningley Road: the Leeds Corporation Tramways depot operated from around 1908 although the first trams ran to Town End in 1902.

Bramley Library was opened July 1927 by the Earl of Elgin and Kincardine, and the Lord Mayor, Alderman Hugh Lupton J.P. As its Chairman, the Earl represented the Carnegie United Kingdom Trust, financed by the Scottish-American industrialist and philanthropist Andrew Carnegie. It was one of the 3,000 Carnegie Libraries he set up in the UK and USA and countries in what was then the British Empire. The first in the UK was opened in 1883 in his home town of Dunfermline. The deal was that Carnegie would build and equip, but only on condition that the local authority matched that cost by providing the land and a budget for operation and maintenance. Typically they comprised a lending library, reference library and newspaper reading room.

Bell Round a typical row of Bramley houses. Bramley had famous sons and daughters: Mary Gawthorpe, suffragette, socialist, trade unionist and editor, lived and worked in Bramley as a school teacher; Ernie Wise, of Morecambe and Wise, was born in Bramley and brought up in East Ardsley; Jamie Peacock MBE, English professional rugby league footballer who played for Leeds Rhinos and Bradford Bulls in the Super League, and captained both Great Britain and England at international level, was born in Bramley in 1977.

Bramley Carnival dates back to around 1865 but the first official carnival was held in 1892. Its origins lie in the Friendly Society Walks which were an annual event in the 19th century. There were a number of friendly societies in the town and on one occasion in the mid 1800s it is said that two society walks met head on in Town Street, with the bands at the head of each parade trying to outplay each other. This has gone down in history as the 'Bramley Clash' and is the ancestor of the Carnival.

Although the street shelter and the people sheltering in it were unscathed, the air raid of August 27th-28th 1942 badly damaged 8 Nansen Grove. The house was occupied by Mr. and Mrs. Arthur Stockhill and their daughters Joan and Jill. Arthur Stockhill was the local air raid warden and was one of the first people to try to salvage some possessions from the burning house. After the raid Joan and Jill spent the rest of the night with neighbours at No. 9. The family were subsequently re-housed on the Wyther Park Estate. The poster urges 'Use less Water'. Thanks to B. Brown on Leodis for the detail. There was an earlier raid on Bramley on the night of August 31st 1940; a bomb exploded on allotments in Outgang. During the course of the war 77 Leeds people were killed and 197 buildings were destroyed with 7,623 damaged, and subsequently repaired, in nine raids. There were 24 major fires. March 14th-15th 1941 saw Leeds's most devastating raid, the so-called 'Quarter Blitz' after the tonnage of bombs dropped. The City was hit repeatedly and was quickly ablaze… 65 people including eight children died that night and a further 258 were injured.

Pollard Lane at the point where the bridge takes it over the Airedale and Wharfedale railway line; other bridges on the lane spanned the Aire and the Leeds and Liverpool Canal. One of Bramley's darkest moments was the murder in 1809 of local girl Rebecca Perigo by Mary Bateman, who was allegedly a witch but no one was taking any chances: she was hanged at York and her corpse given up for dissection at Leeds General Infirmary. Bits of her skeleton were displayed in the Thackray Museum for some years.

The now demolished Lido Cinema, formerly Bramley Picture Palace, opened in 1912 in Town Street to seat 520 people. It was built by Hobson Brothers who operated from Hobson's Yard off Upper Town Street. It closed in March 1961 with its last film *The Nudist Story* starring B Martin. When the films were 'silents' Herbert Appleyard played the piano for many years. When 'talkies' came the cinema was refurbished and the name changed to the Lido in 1931. Disinfectant was sprayed all over during the interval. *Sons of the Saddle* with Ken Maynard was a Western film directed by Harry Joe Brown; on the gable end a poster advertises *Outside the Law* (1930) starring Mary Nolan and Edward G. Robinson. Other popular names for the Lido included 'The Bug Hutch' and 'Loppy-de-Luxe'.

Another Bramley cinema was the up-market Clifton which was in the Art Deco style. The 1,312 seater Clifton Cinema opened on Monday 30th January 1939 with *Woman Against Woman* starring Herbert Marshall, Virginia Bruce and Mary Astor, and also *The Case of the Missing Blonde* with Preston Foster and Patricia Ellis. The Clifton Cinema had a 30 feet wide proscenium and was equipped with Western Electric (WE) sound system. It closed as a cinema on 17th June 1961 with *Carry On Regardless* starring Sid James and Liz Frazer and became a Do-It-Yourself centre, called Howarth Forest Products with signs for the sale of hardwood, softwood, plywood and wallboard (as here).

The five storey Wellington Mill in 1910. Also known as Yates's Mill, this has been the site of a mill since at least 1830. It seems that the original owners were Messrs. Barker and Musgrave for their woollen business; the mill was destroyed by fire in 1830. William Edward Yates (b. 1843) purchased the mill in 1882 for woollen and worsted, having started his cloth manufacturing business in 1871 in Laisterdyke. Yates was an early philanthropist, building three storey houses for his workers with a bathroom on the top floor and outside WC shared by two families. There was also a fish shop and a grocers for the residents and a play area for children. After his death in 1896, he was succeeded by his sons, firstly James Yates and then Charles Yates, and later by his grandsons W.E. Yates and A. Yates. 1899 saw the mill razed again but it rose once more and an artesian well was sunk which produced 12,000 gallons of water per hour. The new chimney, 150 foot tall, is nick-named 'The Duke'. Yates expanded with mills at Armley and with St. Catherine's nearby. In the 1930s they enjoyed a worldwide reputation with agencies in 26 countries.

Gibson's Tannery has its origins in 1902 when Simeon Gibson and Charles Granville Gibson teamed up as tanners and curriers at Hare Park Mills in Hough End with 70 employees. Fire destroyed the mill in 1918 and led to a complete rebuild; by the 1930s they were the biggest tanners in the British Empire. They turned out Glazed Kid leather every year from 2.5 million skins. Kidskin or kid leather is a type of soft, thin leather that is traditionally used for gloves, hence 'kid gloves,' used since at least 1888 as a metaphor for careful handling. It is traditionally made from goatskin – more specifically, the skin of young goats or 'kids'. Glacé or glazed kid has a very glossy, shiny finish.

Upper Town Street. A wonderfully atmospheric streetscape postcard with the obligatory children, this time with dog. All the boys are, typically, wearing hats, and would continue to do so for the rest of their lives. Town Street was home to a number of grand houses, including Bramley Hall, as photographed by Alfred Mattison who was born in Hunslet in 1868. His passion for local history led to a career in lecturing, photography and writing. In 1908 he wrote *The Romance of Old Leeds* based on his articles and photos for the *Yorkshire Daily Observer*. He died following a street accident in Leeds in September 1944.

Ten postmen and a telegraph boy outside Bramley's Town Street post office. The postmen would empty the post boxes and take the letters back to the post office in red painted wicker baskets on wheels where they were pigeon-holed by destination. The post office opened in 1857; post master was Mr. Dawson – he and his son were still running the business in 1900. The postal telegraph was installed in 1871; the telegraph office was open from 8.00am to 8.00pm daily and 8.00am to 10.00am Sundays.

Over the years Bramley has had five different stations in five different locations – four on the Aire Valley Line between Bradford and Leeds which opened in 1846. This is Bramley Railway Station in the early 1900s, looking south from the junction of Stanningley Road and Swinnow Road, seen on the left passing under the railway line. The goods shed is visible on the right, and the footbridge leading to the opposite platform. The station opened in 1854 on the GNR Leeds, Bradford & Halifax line to give a quicker route between the two cities via Bramley; it closed in 1966. A new unmanned station opened on the east side of Swinnow Road in 1983, and the old buildings were demolished.

Another view looking south-east along the platform at Bramley Railway Station. On the north side are the station buildings with separate ladies and gentlemen's waiting rooms. The footbridge crosses the platform where there is another waiting room. Victoria Woollen Mills is in the background. The other bridge leads to Elder Road. October 1872 was a sad day for the town when John Mills, a platelayer oiling points at Bramley, was hit by a passenger train and killed on the spot. Newlay Station was opened in 1846 by the Midland Railway Company. Its route was from Leeds to Shipley Junction where it divided: one arm went to Bradford, the other to Scotland.

Shires Organ Pipes manufacture, repair and restore metal organ pipes. This hefty rounding block is more than 100 years old – but remains in daily use. It displays the stamped signatures of A Calthorpe, W Dickinson, J J Warr and C Shires. John Warr still works at Shires Organ Pipes and this was among the tools he gave to the youngest name on the block, Chris Shires when he began as an apprentice. The rounding block is for making smaller organ pipes round, by placing them on small mandrells, laying them in the rounding block and beating them round. Shires Organ Pipes still trades today in Bramley at Spence Mills, Mill Lane; the firm was founded by Terry Shires when F.J. Rogers of Town Street closed in the 1980s; Terry had been at Rogers since 1975. Examples of their work can be seen at Rikkyo University in Japan and Auckland Cathedral in New Zealand. In 2013 they provided 1,300 pipes for the new OBE Chapel organ in St. Paul's Cathedral where recipients of the OBE and their families can be married and baptised. The firm still uses tools made over 100 years ago to provide organ pipes to those who prefer the original and real thing to the cheaper digital organs available now.

The picture on the left shows a 42-year-old John Warr, now in his early 80s, cupping pipe toes.

The Old Unicorn Inn is marked on the OS Map of Bramley for 1890. It was built from stone quarried at Bramley Falls. An old date stone, in the outdoor seating area, shows the year '1877'; this may have been when the present building was built. On Lower Town Street a date stone is carved with the words 'The Old Unicorn Up this Yard 1877'. This is where the fruiterer Edward St. Quentin of 137 Lower Town Street stabled his horse in the 1940s. The pub, or an earlier one named The Old Unicorn, which possibly dated from the 18th century, is recorded in a local directory published in 1822, when John Firth was landlord. The 18th century wall topped with railings is Grade II listed and has two niches, one of which housed a drinking trough and the other a cast iron water pump with a lion-mask handle and tray. This was the original Bramley water supply until 1927; the pump mechanism is still visible. Not unnatural concern over the purity of the water came from the fact that the water drained from the burial ground. The Water Council eventually replaced it with a main pipe. There was another well at the bottom of Warrel's Road where it was pumped out and flowed down to Waterloo Mill. Another, the Peppy Well, was opposite Gibson's tannery.

Town Street, with Sagar Musgrave's Row and Sagar Musgrave's Place nearby, named after a family of maltsters and landowners: Richard Hartley Sagar was a Bramley solicitor who married Margaret Musgrave of Bramley. Their son, John (1835-1906) added the name Musgrave from his mother's side to his surname to fulfil a condition of inheritance of his great-uncle Abraham Musgrave's fortune. John ran Musgrave and Sagar's brewery at Kirkstall; their Bramley offices can be seen here in the three-storey building on the left. They were established in 1793 as maltsters and brewers; brewing came to an end in 1958 but they continued as bottlers and as a free house chain. Town Street could also boast these pubs: Barley Mow, Star and Garter, Unicorn, Grapes, Cardigan Arms, New Inn. The Star and Garter opened at 6.00 am to serve the workers at Hallidays boot makers with a 2d tot of rum to set them up for the day; on Mondays some stayed all day on what then became Cobbler's Monday. The 17th century Cardigan Arms was terminus for the coach service to the Griffin Hotel in Leeds and horse sales in the yard controlled by the notorious 'Forty thieves' gang who were adept at doctoring old horses to sell there. The Grapes, opposite Stocks Hill, had its own brewery on Town Street.

The three-storey, stone built block to the left comprises Nos. 145 to 147A, which was the premises of James Blakey, photographer; examples of his work are displayed in the window. Moving right, No. 147 is a branch of the Leeds Permanent Society. Next, there are the entrance gates for a garage, advertising the repair of motor cars and motor cycles. After the gates there is the end of a row of stone-built, three-storey houses, now demolished, numbering 149 to 155 Lower Town Street. Nos. 153 and 155 appear to have once been part of one, large Georgian style house. Behind, there is a painted sign on the wall of a pair cottages, advertising the Unicorn Inn for Beers, Wines and Spirits. These cottages were demolished in 1936 to make way for road improvements to Bramley Town Street.

Town Street and part of Stanningley Road form Stanningley's commercial centre. There are ten public houses in Stanningley, including The Jug & Barrel, Waggon & Horses and The Great Northern. In 1781, much of the area around Stanningley was moorland. Joseph Strickland built the first steam-powered mill around 1794 which over time was variously called Company Mill, Temperance Mill, and finally Spring Valley Mill. Stanningley seemed destined to become another West Riding textile village, but its industrial future lay in engineering: factories and mills included Spring Valley Mill, Stanningley Iron Works, Albion Iron Works, Prospect Works, Carrick Foundry, Boot Factory and New Foundry. It all started when Bradford man John Rogers built a small foundry just east of Company Mill before 1827. Rogers died soon after and his widow, Elizabeth, sold the foundry to Charles Haley, Jonas Haley, George Taylor and Joseph Butler in 1830 and the firm became known as Stanningley Iron Works. An inspirational Joseph Pitts joined and by the 1840s Pitts and Butler predicted a huge demand for bridges and other railway structures; they were determined to win as large a slice of the market as possible. Early contracts included a bridge to carry the Lancashire and Yorkshire Railway over Wakefield Road at Bradford in 1850 and the breathtaking roof and the pillars supporting the roof for York Railway Station. By 1861 Butler and Pitts were employing 520 men. Albion Works built and repaired bridges and in the Great War made almost all the plating for British tanks. The metal was tested by firing guns at it in a nearby disused quarry. In the Second World War, munitions were the order of the day including tank parts and bulletproof plating.

Town Street with the Sun Hotel near right opposite the Old Travellers Rest.

Town Street near the junction with Sunfield and Spring Valley and the London City & Midland Bank at No. 1 Town Street next to the Old Traveller's Rest Inn, licensee Joseph Clayburn, at No. 3. Virtually opposite was the Sun Inn at the junction with Richardshaw Lane; licensee William Henry Moore. Then there was the Stanningley & District Working Men's Coal Association at No. 2 Town Street.

Eleven Lane Ends, Stanningley – something looks unfinished here… A section of the A647 Stanningley Road and Stanningley By-Pass became the UK's first High Occupancy Vehicle Lane in 1998. The project was part of an EU research project called Increasing CAR Occupancy (ICARO). Its objectives were to increase car occupancy by encouraging car sharing and to demonstrate the feasibility of providing a lane for shared use by buses, other high occupancy vehicles, motorcycles and cycles. Stanningley is home to the unique Bootie Folding Cycle made by a local engineering firm, F & T Kitchin & Co, at their Vickersdale works as a sideline to their main business. Production of the Bootie bicycle began in 1965 and continued until early 1973.

This tram accident took place on December 12th 1912. The photo shows what was left of Eastmans Ltd, butchers, at 1A Bradford Road, when a tram smashed into the frontage. In the centre is a man holding an Eastmans sign for the camera – or maybe the insurance claim!

Tram no. 281 was the culprit: here it is after it had left the rails and crashed into the shop.

George Cohen Sons & Co. Ltd, converted to war work in the Second World War in their factory in Town Street. The business first saw the light in 1843 when George Cohen opened a scrap and ship-building business in the south of England. In 1876 it relocated to 600 Commercial Road in East London and in 1929 moved to Stanningley on premises and land previously occupied by John Butler & Co. Ltd, iron roof manufacturers, at 118–126 Town Street. Between 1939 and 1945 bombs and shells were manufactured here by a workforce of over 350, many of whom were temporary men, i.e. women. The Stanningley site covered an area of 14 acres and was, in its prime, one of the largest steel stockholders in the country, taking surplus metals from British Steels mills at Bromford, Wednesbury, Clydesdale, Hartlepool and Corby. The machine tool side of the 600 Group closed on the Stanningley site in 1987, but a subsidiary of the 600 Group GCS (Steels) Ltd continued to operate there until October 1999. George Cohen Sons & Co. Ltd had registered as the '600 Group Ltd' in 1975 and has since evolved into the largest machine tool company in the U.K. Here, a female employee can be seen welding the tubular framework of a nacelle for an Anson aircraft. She wears safety goggles, an overall, a leather apron and trousers as she undertakes this traditionally male occupation. Women formed a "skilled and reliable workforce" nationwide during the Second World War.